KATY BRIDGE

Saint Julian Press

Poetry

Praise for KATY BRIDGE

"The past comes to me," writes David Watts in one of the many excellent poems in *Katy Bridge*. And indeed, it does. In poems both meditative and ruminative, Watts helps readers see what he sees and feel what he feels when he is visited by particularly poignant memories. When merged with candid observations from the present, *Katy Bridge* becomes a kaleidoscope of invention and experience we are all invited to look through.

— Dean Rader
Winner of the T. S. Eliot Prize for Poetry

These are tender poems that encompass a physician/poet's lifetime—memories of school and first girlfriends of serious love and physical loving of presences and absences, of the mysteries and revelations of the human body—poems that linger at the borders of our beautiful and ever-changing natural world. He is a poet of spot-on and evocative images, a poet who has touched death and so can show us how to rejoice in the living, finally reassuring us that "every small leaving is tender." Here, we find moments of humor tinged with sorrow, sorrow tinged with joy, gifted to us in poems sparkling and accomplished.

— Cortney Davis
Taking Care of Time and *Daughter*

A deep abiding tenderness courses through David Watts' latest collection *Katy Bridge.* With grace and precision, the poet places us right there on the bridge beside him, where "walking the rails gets a tad different with trestles on either side. Always a train somewhere up the tracks." Here is the radiant present, perfectly expressed, and the bridge becomes both memory and metaphor. These wise, wide-awake poems reveal each moment as a bridge between past and future, the body as a bridge between mysteries, and love as a bridge between solitudes. Like stones "rounded by the watery sandpaper of the ocean" and "polished . . . with my thumb, withdrawing some element of me upon them, shiny as a blessing," these poems seem to be patiently shaped by the process of living in this world, then polished in the rare luminosity of Watts' vision. This is a book to savor and return to.

— Erin Rodoni
And If The Woods Carry You
Winner of The Southern Indiana Review Michael Waters Poetry Prize

KATY BRIDGE

Poems

by

David Watts

SAINT JULIAN PRESS
HOUSTON

Published by
SAINT JULIAN PRESS, Inc.
2053 Cortlandt, Suite 200
Houston, Texas 77008

www.saintjulianpress.com

COPYRIGHT © 2023
TWO THOUSAND AND TWENTY-THREE
© David Watts

ISBN-13: 978-1-955194-22-8
Library of Congress Control Number: 2023946658

Cover Art Credit: David Watts & Ron Starbuck

To my parents, Harvey and Lillian, who set the stage.

CONTENTS

Katy Bridge	1
Swimming with Edith	2
Dealing with Brian	3
Hanging the Birdhouse	5
Supermoon	7
Afterprint	8
Two Deer in Early Morning	10
Absence and a Deep Mirror	12
After January 1st	14
Returning Home	15
At Night	16
Fear and Resilience	17
This Poem is Curious	18
Eyeblink	19
Marilyn on the Wall of the Cedar Choppers Bar	20
Love by its Own Plan	23
Water	24
Piece of Bone	25
In the Pause of Morning	27
Conversations	28
Sycamore	30
Waiting for My Colonoscopy	31
Death Sequence	32
Since You Will Leave Me or I will Leave You	38
Five Stones	40

Walking to School Late Autumn	42
Necessary	43
Solstice, Winter	44
Empty Bedroom	45
Abundance	47
Father, Son and Dishes in the Sink	49
In Banff	51
Solstice, Summer	52
Jenner Stones	53

PREFACE

sine qua non

I came to poetry out of necessity. I wasn't any good at it at right away. Even so, it lifted me from darkness. But it said to me, "If you're going to make poems you better know what you are doing." Thus began a long preparation which brought me here. Sharon Olds told me, "If you love poetry long enough it will love you back." She was right.

I have learned that poetry is a demanding bedmate. A rosy addiction. It will purify your life, sometimes painfully. It will abandon you if you hedge at the cusp of danger. It requires more courage than you have. Borrowing its levers and sprockets to crank out a personal version of beauty demands a whole continent of attention.

Your soul may grow wings but truth has its burdens. In place of complacent bliss it gives you a stormy life. You are aware. Your nerve endings flare. You are flotsam in the riptide of love.

So now, this book—a mix of old and new, gentle and harsh—is a search for the convergence of truth and beauty. The honesty is at times embarrassing but necessary, for the reward it gives is an occasional flash of exhilarating insight.

The astonishment is, after all, that the process is sometimes more valuable than the product. Yet what stands after all is a marker to the struggle to know ourselves and make of this life something deeper.

As it turns out, diving into the interior opens the universe.

David Watts
Mill Valley, California
September 2023

"... what, anyway, was that sticky infusion, that rank flavor of blood, that poetry, by which I lived?"

—Galway Kinnell

KATY BRIDGE

KATY BRIDGE

Rumored to be a Lover's Leap over shallow water. Home of ghosts.
River running low in summer.

Thought I remembered standing next to the girders one time,
pressed flat by the bellow of a passing train.

Turned sideways to the eyes of an awkward death that lured me there,
foolishly there. I ignored his stare and didn't die.

Never sure I really did that. The bridge probably made it up where memories
splatter like oil on the rails. Mostly,

it was a place to take your girlfriend for a scare, a kiss and a dare
and beat it when the rails start to shake.

Rare seasons I had one. Girlfriend, that is. Scary thought: trains and girlfriends.
What I can say is that walking rails gets a tad different

with trestles on either side of you. Always a train somewhere up the tracks
headed your way, the rails alive like snakes slithering,

the 4 o' clock hissing its way down from Waco.

SWIMMING WITH EDITH

Aroma of water drying
on limestone.

Rope swing. A tangled oak.
They said Blue Hole

was so deep you couldn't see
the bottom. Swimming over it

was your body wanting to sink
into infinity.

Pickles and awful pimento
cheese sandwiches. Love infantile

as an unhatched egg.
Her shy body

trying on shapes. Both of us
wanting something.

DEALING WITH BRIAN

Odd, the way we gathered after Brian's funeral,
        like a cluster of awkward parishioners on Easter Sunday.

    Late summer light piercing the dark windows.

I watched to see how my friends handled the shock:
           Johnny, matter-of-fact about how Brian fell from
   the tower,

Margaret weeping—I couldn't tell what kind of tears they were—
        Julie working a gi-normous bowl of ice cream and I,

thinking we were being too insincere,
          too indifferent to the moment's heft,

      lying about our feelings. Planning what to do when
school
    started again.

          We should have been more careful
    not to embarrass Brian
              and make him feel sad about
  being dead like that,

      his absence a faint presence drifting in the room.

   I couldn't tell how I should feel about this: Julie

     digging away in the milky graveyard of an ice cream mound,

bored with the whole event,

                perhaps impatient to go buy school supplies, or

    do anything a bit more exciting,

our minds shifting from the obligation of sorrow

      to an imaginary time where the horror of teen-age death would be one more day behind us.

        "Don't go see him," his mother said. "That's not Brian."

I was glad not to, preferring to remember him turning loops with his
        model airplane, playing solos on his trombone,

driving his blue '47 glass pack loud-as-hell Ford coupe, hunched
      over the steering wheel, duck tails slicked back in the wind.

    We stood awkwardly a while,
            then disbanded.

    Some played washers in the back yard, others
  went to the river to swim.

      Some waited around, unsure what to do,

others stared hard into the face of the future.

HANGING THE BIRDHOUSE

I admit it.
More for me than the bird.

Yet how could she not
like the dormer windows,
the yellow clapboards, the little

fake flowers in the little fake
windowboxes—country living
in a teeny tiny house.

I fashion a hook from a coathanger,
extend myself outrageously
from my deck, swaying
in the wind so as

to match the sway of the tree
to hang perfectly
the perfectly-adjusted crook
over the perfectly-chosen

branch and then, not satisfied,
tweak it three times,

and then,
because it's not quite right, replace it
three more times

to get the face facing forward
so it looks just great out my window.

That bird's gonna love it.

SUPERMOON

The moon dipped low

and pushed through the branches.

I was lucent

in my night robe.

There was a quick owl

in the shadow place

where grace and danger

are the same

as a swift death.

Beautiful to die

under silent wings.

The woods deepen

where the moon can't reach

made of shadows

and frozen light.

AFTERPRINT

She rises from the bed
leaving a swirl in the sheets
the shape of her leaving,

afterprint of ridges and folds
her body makes
lifting from mine. I imagine

a slip of air still moving
where she passed the foot of the bed
on her way to coffee

and the morning news.
Much is about departure,
one moment dying

into the next as we wake
and move
into another day as if

it would be always the same. Yet,
riding in the hollows
there is this tugging like geese

pulling southward.
A moment trembles,
then it fades. But the heart

propels it
where the strings of memory
are stored. The morning

fresh against the stale
patina of sleep. The air
disturbed in layers.

Everything tender
about this moment gone.
And still here.

TWO DEER IN EARLY MORNING

They came to my back door.
    The mother,
        tall and slender.
            A smudge of grey.

    And the small one
        a speckled fawn,
            neither confident nor afraid.

They were munching my green grass
    their furry kingdom close enough
        to reach into.

        I could almost stroke
        their ears,
            delicate as a breath.

What would it be like to move with grace
    the way they do
        gliding among the narrow trees?

            To dissolve in forests and reappear without regret
or sorrow.

If I stand very still they will go back to chewing a tuft of summer grass.

    If I move,

    the fawn will turn her fire-streaked eyes on me
            asking to know me
                        for who I am.

          Conversation   just a heartbeat,
                                          not spoken.
Then,

      the moment changes.

           For something has been watching

    from the forest

                    and reaches now

          to draw them back

as if their world had waited too long

                        to call them home,

     as if they were never here.

ABSENCE AND A DEEP MIRROR
after Leila Chatti

Your trench coat
hangs on hooks in the hall. Your absence
drifts like smoke through the rooms.

Emptiness reliable
as the ache of a broken bone.

The mirror is an open eye I stand before, naked, watched
as you watched me from across the bed.

I don't know how I learned to be so undressed,
so hungry. Skin-memory rising
like a chill.

Hours with your eyes angular, as if
ordained. The small hairs of my chest imbedded

in the reach of your heartbeat
the way the wind claims mimosa.

You made me a thing imagined.

You said you would stay as long as we were worthy.
Moments rose like corridors swelling.

We were the echo of that song.

Light from the street
slips its fingers into my shadow.
The mirror is ravenous.

I am the hollow reflection of your departure.

AFTER JANUARY 1ST

Strong winds, a clarity of light
precise as an etching.

I shun pasta for oats,
exercise like it matters

and I, too,
have a new clarity.

Alone, more age seeps in.
Time too short

for regret. The calm
around me so alive

that solitude
is a drop of honey.

I clean house better
now that I have to.

Cirrus white against
a Giotto sky. Cold nights.

Whatever I've lost I release
to this articulate light.

RETURNING HOME

The Hackberries were gone,
replaced by cottonwood
and pecan

and the house of many echoes
was smaller
deflated by absence.

The spaces were still there
but could not be entered.

And what of love? What
can replace what is thinned out
over long distances?

The sunlight more vertical, now,
the wind the same wind

pushing cottonwood tufts
out to the horizon.

AT NIGHT

The past comes to me
and says what it wants:
a firestone bike,
a lost girlfriend.

They exist only as I dream them
yet the past wants me to stand
outside my mind where the bicycle

and the girlfriend still live,
where the past is a different past
now that memory shapes it
the way it wants.

These images are unruly.
They change even as I hold them tightly,
even as I claim what I can
as mine.

FEAR AND RESILIENCE
for Alina

In the dream
there is a boat crossing the pond
that has lost its passengers.

The oars languish untended
in their locks. And there is
this unstable, rocking feeling.

A knock on the sill and the dream
wakes the dreamer. She finds
fear occupying every cell in her body.

Her ribs squeeze her heart.
Her breathing narrows to a whisper.
Her legs tangle in worries

and pond reeds.
She remembers how as a child
she would call out

and her mother would rise
to bring the perfect words.
She calls them to her ears

and with each deep breath
she pulls the oars
firmly through the unsteady waters.

THIS POEM IS CURIOUS

The first time that sex was truly fantastic was when I risked everything.
    It was not about love. And it was about love.

The hillside was doing that thing I liked, waving its hair in the wind.
    I wasn't paying attention to the hillside.

You turned to me like a promise. I read the architectures of your body.
    You collected my tears in the teacup of your collarbone.

The secret we owned, owned us. Our ecstasy was the hope
    of hope fulfilled. Tugged many ways, the body took its own path.

Delicious was the tension between our world and the other world. How it
    brushed our bones with silver. How there was no other world.

I thought I saw someone at the window. You made me forget.
    Part of me died right then. Part of me joined another kingdom.

EYEBLINK
after Rumi

I heard your laughter.
Now I have a secret life.

I tasted the honey of your tongue
and my life traded places with itself.

There are things about this transaction
I cannot tell anyone.

But see how the breath off your hand
is all that separates us, space, not a space

where the unsayable hides. Already,
I have spoken the happiness of your name.

I have lived the mountains and rivers of your body.
What I know is what I didn't know

five minutes ago. And it doesn't even
have a name.

MARILYN ON THE WALL AT THE CEDAR CHOPPER'S BAR

Sammy's dad took us to The Cabin.
We must have been fifty miles
west of Waco on this puddle called a lake.

The boys nosed around the woods
like boys will do,
exploring the strange territories of Hill Country,
ramped up by the fear of poison ivy
and rattlesnakes.

We talked about Rodney
who was already smoking and Ginger
who was growing tits, and then
Sammy's dad badly needed a beer.

So we all went down the road to the Cedar Chopper's Bar.

"Never call it Cedar Chopper's," said his dad,
"or risk having something valuable
chopped off."

He ordered two bottles of Jax
and we got cokes.

There was an unfinished Schlitz
on the next table and I said Rodney
would probably drink that beer.

Sammy didn't think so,
and right then we saw Marilyn on the wall, life-sized
and proportional
in that terrifying way that made my balls crimp.

Her back was toward us, but her face
turned back, smiling, as if to say,
"Check this out."

And we did, actually:
her bright eyes, her shy breast pointing out
like a mainsail.

And I saw the smudge on her butt-cheek
from a thousand love pats no one dares in real life,
nuzzles from sticky, cedar-sapped hands as they passed out the door.

It gave those Cedar-Choppers strength, I bet.
Gave them
a piece of a dream they needed to push back deep

into the cedar thicket, nicked and scratched,
pasted all over with the sticky gum of angry, sap-oozing branches.

Must have made a life of slender hopes
almost bearable.

Sammy's dad said we had to go before the fistfights began,
so we left. But Marilyn's soft blue eyes
caught me watching her as I moved to the door.
I heard her say she didn't mind.

And then, Well, I couldn't help myself.

I reached over and patted that round, wonderful ass

leaving my very own, teen-age smudge of deepest, soulful reverence,
miserable in love.

LOVE BY ITS OWN PLAN

I gave a girl a buffalo nickel.
I wanted it to wear thin
in the pocket of her skirt.

She spent it.
Made a worry nickel
out of me, passing

my love through the fingers
of many girls, dissolving
me into bits of myself,

the girls rubbing
their thumbs against
my face

for love's dusty residue.

WATER
> *after Shelly Wong*

Sometimes words are like numbers
in a tumble cage. Sometimes rain
that whispers in trees.
Sometimes stone. I don't know why
I left Galveston. Maybe part of me
loves tingle and the undertow.
I saw a pony that was dapple gray
and it reminded me of branches in sunlight.
And the way after rain the streets
turn to mirrors. The sun bouncing.
I could be the droplets in trees
that bend light.
My eyes, useful fluids.
The nouns I write spell the past
before it evaporates
or maybe scatters among leaves.
Maybe a lightpath
on bay waters just after moonrise
above the Berkeley hills.
Images tight
as affections between the letters
of a poem.
Welcome, moon.
Welcome, bay.
Welcome sunshine, twice reflected.

PIECE OF BONE

I suspect it was vertebra,

twin domes of articulation
like the split roof of an observatory.

Eyeholes for the escape of nerves
from the—I presume there was one—
spinal cord. Held just right

it was a skull that could look at you
from any point in the room—some
small prehistoric marsupial, perhaps,

with teeth curved like a wart hog.
Found it scuffing around
a dusty bone pile, tossed in

with a bunch of cedar scraps
someone had chipped
out west of Austin. Jumped

into my vision like a burning bush,
only there wasn't one.
Slipped it on my neckerchief

instead of those burnished
square knots most Scouts wear—caused
a lot of questions I didn't

have answers for. Loved
the mystery of that
and the distinction of it,

and the crackerjack anomaly
that it was. As if a piece of bone
said something about me

I didn't know myself.
Stayed with me all the way
to the Eagle Scout photo

Mrs. Cluck took with her camera
that looked like a space station.
She's gone.

The photo's gone.
And the little skull
which probably wasn't a skull. . .

let's just say
it found its way back to the bone pile
where no one asks its name.

IN THE PAUSE OF MORNING

You roll to the edge of the bed and sit quietly
        in the rising light.

I was awake before you, remembering
        the first time.

I watched you, then, rolling naked
        to the edge.

    I said love died in me. And I wondered if we would couple.
           "Not if, but when," you said
    and walked straight into my longing.

Old ideas fell like shards of a discredited truth.
    The night convulsed.

You made a liar out of me.

CONVERSATIONS
for Gabriel

I will tell you how I read. I don't read. I remember.

Sometimes when I can't get to sleep it's because the body isn't tired enough to
    develop a dream.

Hey, Dad. Did you know that there's thirty percent gravity in your head, and that's
    why your brain floats?
Where'd you get that idea?
I don't know. I just made it up.

Dad, I discovered something.
Yeah?
You can't see a shadow from something that gives off light.

I was asleep and I opened my eyes to see if I was awake.
I ran out of dream power. Can I go ask mom if she has any?

You say NCIS is running out of material? How can a crime show run out of ideas?
    Just hire someone with a dark mind.

Hey Dad, come look. All I did was drop these sticks and I made a Sardini glass.
A what?
A Sardini glass. Come look.
Oh, you mean Martini glass.
Martini, Sardini. . . these adults are so precise.

Did you know that if you sit real still you can feel the earth move?
It's like sitting on a spring-mounted platform waiting for it to push you up.
Only slower.

Dad, when did you buy this tamale?
A long time ago.
That's not a long time ago. I was not born a long time ago.

SYCAMORE

A woman sits on her bed
by the window watching
the great sycamore.
Her crying is a secret

alive inside her. Whatever
she tells him,
however she says it,
she will remain unknown.

They search for answers
in the forests of their bodies
as winter works the last leaves.

He tries to find her
inside the mystery
while she watches colors
and thinks of ancestors.

He is looking for a language
that will shape
the silence between them.
The heart wobbles and yearns.

The sycamore accepts
the oncoming winds,
bends a little,
and drops what it has to the ground.

WAITING FOR MY COLONOSCOPY

I am narrow.
A man without feet.

Trunked into this hospital bed
without my atmospheres.

I speak my surface self
with surface words

that have short roots.
My unconscious is an idea

of itself, floating
in its faded image.

What I say has the texture
of sponges with empty

pores. We joke and smile
above the obvious

but the obvious isn't
going anywhere.

DEATH SEQUENCE

To plumb the unknown
to plunge the ear into passage
to uncover the carefully covered stone

And I went to the place
where death was,
to the dying of my friend,
in her white room.

And I said, Death
speak to me. But death
just rustled like leaves
where it passed. . .

Death would not speak
for not being able to
and I could not hear
from the outside
which was covered over.

So I placed myself in the center
of my friend

and rested there, calm,
and quiet.

I had no feeling for what
had made me happy

or sad,

there was just an unwrinkling of the body
spreading out

blanketing a terrain of broad valleys, like water
dissolving into the earth.

I see I have carried death

all along, there
at the bottom of my reach

when I am falling back into myself,
extending my long arms

to scoop up the silt. As a child
death wanted only to be known,

nothing more than that, speaking
to me softly

in dreams: I was the detective
seeking the murderer

hiding under my back steps,
finding pieces of small children

lying around like clues
everybody feared but nobody wanted.

When the murderer saw me
an angel tapped me on the shoulder

and I started to rise

into the light air above the circle of children
watching me.

*

When we went to the apartment
I could see that death
was already there,
even though it wasn't supposed to be.

I could see it in the way things
were arranged on the shelves—the same way
when you go into a house
after someone has died and you say

those things haven't been moved for years—
death was in them.

She wasn't playing it well,
the way she said she didn't know. . .
she might even die—as if
it wasn't going to happen.

It struck me she hadn't given
the same excellence to her death
that she had to her literary criticism
or her grading of papers,
or feeding the cat.

It made me sad to know
she was not equipped for this,
that she might sail right on
to the very end
not believing.

When my mentor was dying
he had more courage
than all of us,
he just caught death
in a sidelong glance
and invited him in for breakfast.

We tried optimisms.
He would have none of it.
We tried hope.
He just sat down with death at the table
and waited.

*

I went back to my friend
and rested inside her.
She was the carriage
for my journey part way.
And I thought

of the poem I wrote
when my son refused us,
how death shows its face
when sorrow comes:

> *A young girl stands at the obedient river.*
> *With her line she spoons the water*

> *for fish. They cannot resist*
> *her darting flashes among the shadows.*

> *How beautiful she is. How beautiful*
> *she makes their death for them.*

> *How refreshing,*

> *finally to give up hope—to give in*
> *to this passionate certainty*

> *that there is nothing I can do*
> *and nothing more I want.*

And my friend said,
I am beginning to think
I am dying . . .

SINCE YOU WILL LEAVE ME OR I WILL LEAVE YOU

Because the light is fading and because
    it has been told to do so
the street lamp
   embers up, embers down, ignition
hesitating at the spark.

      Barely on, barely off, it pulses
in the dying light.

   A little wind,
a tuft of hair drifting, and the shape of a woman
      moves through the forms she takes
    leaving in dusklight—
  I watch

with the same eyes I have watched you
bathing, silken
with sweat and with loving,
my body folded
into yours, as now
   even across this distance
    even against the wind and the light.

     We are older
       and we know love
is eventually about leaving. Isn't it true?

   That is why every small leaving is tender.

    In the road of departure,
still moving like departure,
   halfway into the world
at the edge where two worlds meet
     the woman turns
and looks back
       and the sun,
which used to fade without hesitation,
              snags on its last
  illumination
      orange with longing,
          clinging to the edge of the earth.

FIVE STONES

Five stones sit between the coffee maker
and faucet, tokens I picked up
on Wreck Beach off the straight of water
north of Puget Sound, tossed
and rounded by the watery sandpaper
of the ocean.
I polished them with my thumb,
withdrawing some element of me
upon them, shiny as a blessing.
Now, these stones know something
about me as they glisten quietly
on the counter: one, the countenance of
a gibbous moon, the second, the unstill arc
of Jupiter's stripes,
third, the creamy mildness of a spirit in repose,
then the rose pink of salmon flesh,
and last, a darkness that never speaks.
We walked together on that beach,
you and I, speaking
as lovers do when they remind themselves
their pasts, saying those things
we'd not found time to say, not saying
what no one will ever hear,
cradled in the chambers of two hearts
swelling. Something changed
in that moment, as if no person or thing
could ever be alone in the universe,

the moment opening,
the waves at our feet,
the stones in our hands,
these collected treasures, colorations
of the elements that made us.

WALKING TO SCHOOL, LATE AUTUMN

November cracks the window
with its snowy knife. Smell of ice

and gunpowder.
On the north horizon winter

loads its rage in boxcars
heading south.

I am warm and freezing
in my mackinaw. Coffee belly.

Pencil sharp. My binder of ideas
under my arm, asking

questions. Body straining
toward muscles and desire,

wishing the girl down the street
to my side, reaching for my hand.

NECESSARY

They say we were rich. So fine
between the brunch and the bed.

Some blessings happen without help.
The fern unrolls its fronds.

Hoof prints vanish before the hunter
can follow. We were free from hunters.

In bed, mid morning, the sun
sparkles the curtains with fireflies.

We sipped brilliance and did not die.
Pleasure not earned, but necessary.

Our sorrows giggled among the sheets
and tangled feet. Who were we then

between the shouting and the sunrise?
We decided to name a passing trolley.

You said you liked pomegranate.
I said maple syrup.

We traced our names on the ceiling
and watched them melt away.

SOLSTICE, WINTER

The light is pulling us
toward spring.

Eventually, the high tide
of darkness will ebb

as the Earth spins in
more sun. I don't know why

darkness is so thick, why
Jupiter has to groan so hard

turning on its axis. After rain
fingers of night stretch

and crawl into morning. The sun
just a lingering color

at winter's edge, before
the dawn dawns, before

the window shade pulls back
and there is this deep sigh.

EMPTY BEDROOM

My son's bed made
the same way seven days now,
    folds
in the hand-stitched quilt
also the same,

the shadows they cast
mark the progress of the days. . .

   —cold Augusts
by The Bay,
    the little metastases of winter
into summer—

. . . and his cigarettes on the dresser
in the pack,
hemp tattoo kit,
ear stud. . .

   When his mother calls
and asks what have you accomplished
    he may not know the answer.

maybe that sudden

freedom thing,
like a lock
   off the door.

Girl friend.
    A few mornings
        learning what it's like to wake up
in a lover's bed.

Some pasts stay lived in,
    seed-fragment held on
too long.
      Some broken,
temporarily . . .

I nod my head
    without thinking to do so
        and the nod spins back on me
saying enough, enough, turning me

to the morning paper,
Rice Chex in the bowl—

the commute waiting.

ABUNDANCE

You come to the room
   where we've made love
many times before. You say
   your body has changed.

Outside the rains of winter
   droop green aprons
down the hillside.
   You've always wanted

the windows open,
   light drifting around us
as if from no single source
   as now, not changed,

even after the surgeon's cut
   and the scar the ovary hides
the shape of a baby's fingernail—
   sliver of moon

sliver of last bit of soap
   in the dish
where the egg, sucked
   into the Petri dish

was our last attempt
   to make a life.
You say you've changed.
   It's true.

We both are different,
    but also not
different: we still say
    "It may be cold out.

You should take along
    a pull-over, or
Can you remember where
    I put those blue pillowcases?"

Love is not love that cannot be deepened
    by sorrow—
Let that fish swim where it may—
    You are so beautiful.

FATHER, SON AND DISHES IN THE SINK

"Would you help your father
unload the dishwasher," she says
and Gabriel turns his feet
from the strong magnet
pulling him to the sanctity
of his room where his parallel
universe lives and he will descend
into the unreachable.
He stretches a hand and lifts
a spoon to its place
among the community of spoons
in the drawer.
I squeeze five plates together
to move to the cabinet.
He does the same. I reach
for the mixing bowl and our fingers
touch and my father
is in the spaces between us,
humming his tone deaf tune
as he tilts a glass into
its perfect slip. I have watched
him turn the glass just so
among the elders standing
like sentries on the shelf.
And now my son watches me
imitating the reflection of my father
down through the generations.

Two of us working and
the dishes disappear three times
as fast and he is gone
to his world that pulls him gently
away. It's fine.
He carries with him my father
and me
and more I will never know.

IN BANFF

The wind has been tickling the aspens
all morning. They dodge and shiver.
They can hardly stand it.

Scent of snow off the sudden mountain
and the magpie probes the grass for breakfast.
Last night's opera in my mind, even

my stride is satisfied.
Air thin, aroma of pine, this place
the backstreets of my mind.

SOLSTICE, SUMMER
for Duston

How the light has endurance.
How it filters into the border of night
like milk spilled.

Something wise about this calm,
a distant relative
familiar by strangeness.

I don't want anything.
Not even the comforting numbness
of a schedule.

Just this Adirondack chair
its bony slats against my back.
And the way this day wants to be watched.

JENNER STONES

At Jenner-by-the-Sea we scurry
over boulders to the place
where the breakers bear down,

the edge where rub and thrust
rinses everything finally clear.
It has taken a long time

to get here, past failures at love,
at marriage, but sometimes, after all,
there is an accident of grace.

We are cautious
and treasure everything
in our tennis shoes.

We teeter
over the runnels that rush
between footings, in which,

emptied by the gasp and suck
of the sea collapsing back,
we find the small

stones we came for: freshetts
of color like floral nuggets
compressed to their smallest density.

Jadeite. Feldspar. Serpentine
and the one with an orange-mango cloud
marbling through like a fossilized sunset.

We cannot know where they came from,
though we imagine an ancient vein
glowing under a billion years of sediment

somewhere up the Russian River,
a cliff quarried
by the current's constant fingers,

then fanned from the river's mouth
and tossed on this beach
like jewel-stones left by a passing goddess.

I press them between my thumb
and forefinger. It may not be so bad
to go on for years with nothing

happening, nothing
but the downward heft of sediment—and then
this blossoming!

ACKNOWLEDGEMENTS

Gratitude to the following journals where these poems first appeared:

Juniper   "Afterprint"

Nostos   "Two Deer in Early Morning"
"At Night"

Throats to the Sky   "This Poem is Curious"

Full of Crow   "Piece of Bone"

Justice for All, 2007   "Jenner Stones"

Also,
Cumberland Poetry Review,   A Robert Penn Warren Finalist
The Lascaux Review   A Lascaux Prize Finalist,
The Ina Coolbrith Poetry Prize for Best Love Poem.

NOTES

There are echoes of Jane Hirshfield in "Two Deer in Early Morning," p10, and of Jack Gilbert in "Sycamore" p30.

The poem, "Absence and a Deep Mirror," p12, is working in the style and subject matter of Leila Chatti

"Water" p 24, is a tribute to the artistry of Shelly Wong.

"Waiting for My Colonoscopy" is a written in the voice of my pseudonym, Harvey Ellis.

"Death Sequence" came out of an experiment in which I attempted to project part of my consciousness into that of my dying friend in order, from somewhere inside her, to better understand her plight. Using that experience the poem took its own form and pushed in directions of its own making. It came forth almost without editing.

ABOUT THE AUTHOR

Thirty-four books from the pen of David Watts have been published: short stories, mysteries, westerns, Christmas memoirs, NPR commentaries, haiku, small books of aphoristic wisdoms, translation, and at the heart of it all, poetry. Trained as a physician and classical musician he turned to poetry mid-life and has never turned back. He has led workshops nationally and teaches poetry at the Fromm Institute of San Francisco. His interest in the contribution of the unconscious to the process of creation has led to a body of imaginative work under the pen name, Harvey Ellis, a leaping, associative voice that is to be found as a quiet influence in parts of the current work. His new project is a collection of essays and reflections.

Typefaces Used
GARAMOND – Garamond
PERPETUA TILTING MT – Perpetua Tilting MT